Collins

easy le[arning]

Phonics

quick quizzes

Ages 5–7

ai ? e
oo   th
       ck

Jill Atkins

Missing vowels

Add a vowel letter to make a word to match the picture.

Remember, the vowel letters are a, e, i, o and u.

1. c___t
2. d___g
3. z___p
4. l___g
5. h___t
6. c___p
7. c___p
8. t___n
9. s___n
10. b___d
11. f___x
12. j___m

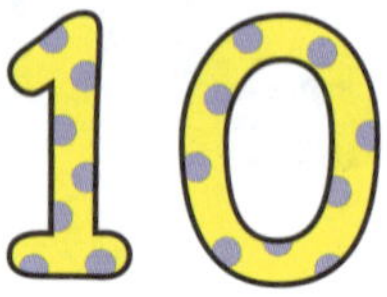

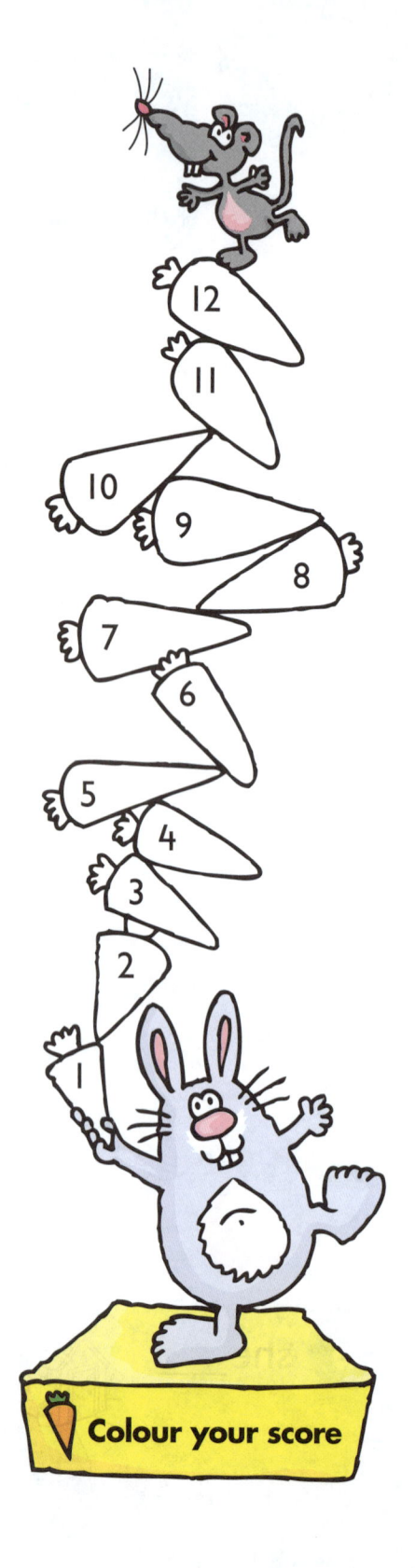

Colour your score

Missing last sound

Add the missing sound to make a word to match the picture.

Some sounds have two letters, like **sh**.

1. li___ 
2. mo___ 
3. we___ 
4. di___ 
5. sa___ 
6. to___ 
7. for___ 
8. she___ 
9. ru___ 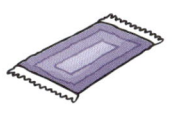
10. shi___ 
11. ma___ 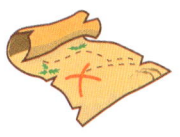
12. we___ 
13. shee___ 
14. ri___ 
15. woo___

Colour your score

x or cks?

Write x or cks at the end to make a word.

1. mi_____
2. jin_____
3. sma_____
4. ki_____
5. bo_____
6. pe_____
7. rela_____
8. lyn_____
9. ta_____
10. qua_____
11. fi_____
12. suffi_____
13. o_____
14. li_____
15. ba_____

A noun ending x is singular. A noun ending cks is plural.

Colour your score

ch, sh or th?

Add ch, sh or th at the beginning to make a word.

Remember, there are two ways to say the th sound.

1. ____em
2. ____ess
3. ____ut
4. ____ed
5. ____ap
6. ____ud
7. ____ree
8. ____all
9. ____imp
10. ____oot
11. ____is
12. ____an
13. ____art
14. ____en

Colour your score

The short e sound

Add e or ea to make a word.

1. m____nt
2. h____n
3. inst____d
4. spr____d
5. j____t
6. w____b
7. h____d
8. y____t
9. br____d
10. t____n
11. thr____d
12. d____d
13. l____mon
14. n____st
15. l____g

If you get any words wrong, use the 'look, say, cover, write, check' method to learn them.

Colour your score

oo words

Sort the words into two groups.

book	took	food	pool
foot	moon	zoo	wood
mood	good	soon	bamboo
boom	cook	broom	

oo makes a short sound, e.g. l**oo**k	**oo** makes a long sound, e.g. sp**oo**n

Say each word out loud to decide where it should go.

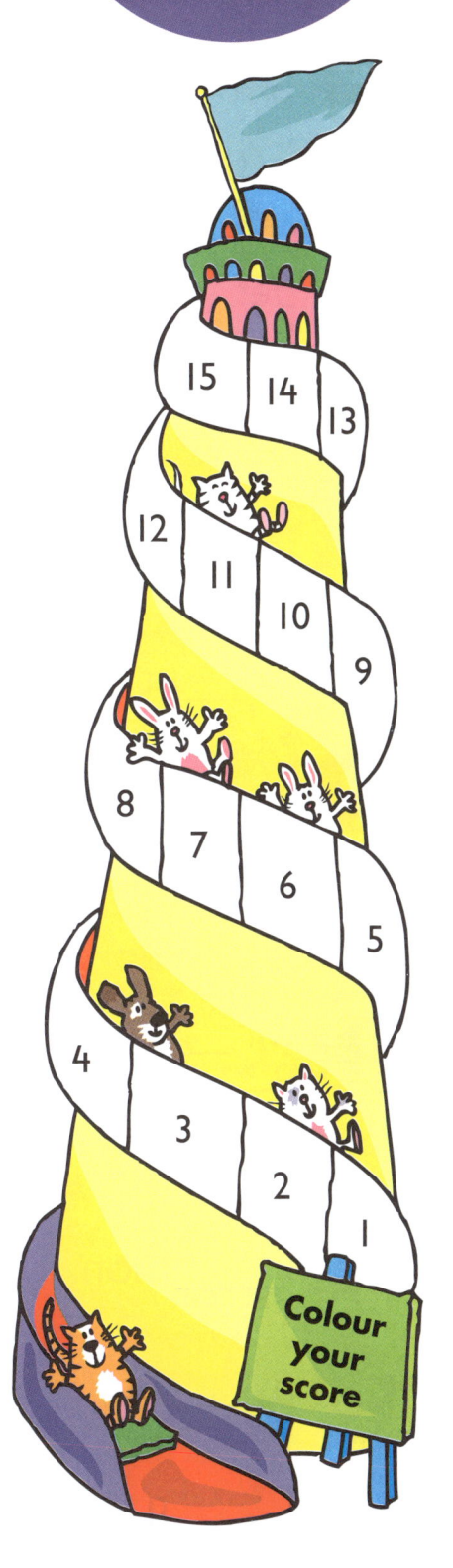

Colour your score

or, ore, aw and au

Add or or ore to make a word.

1. m_____
2. sh_____t
3. b_____n
4. sc_____
5. bef_____
6. h_____se
7. sh_____

Add aw or au to make a word.

8. s_____
9. dr_____
10. _____thor
11. p_____se
12. y_____n
13. astron_____t
14. cr_____l
15. h_____nt

If you get any words wrong, use the 'look, say, cover, write, check' method to learn them.

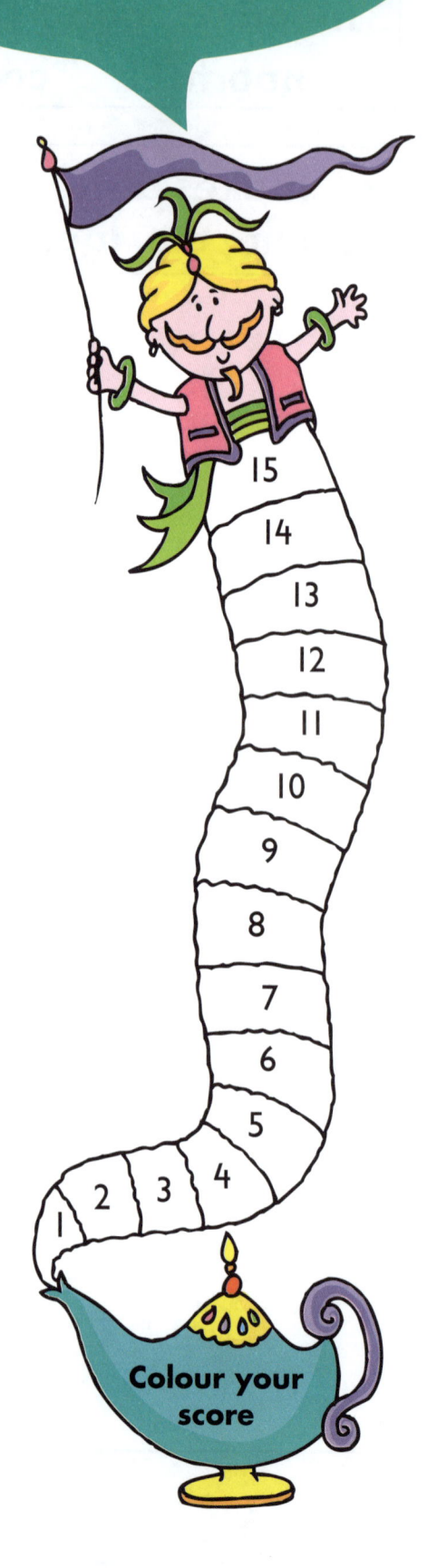

Colour your score

Word endings

Underline the real word in each pair.

1. bank — bamp
2. losh — lock
3. cruss — crust
4. sap — saq
5. wem — well
6. wism — wish
7. park — parg
8. honk — hoch
9. meeb — meet
10. hulp — hulk
11. book — booy
12. boaw — boat
13. desk — desp
14. thank — thand
15. sheeb — sheep

Only one word in each question is a real word.

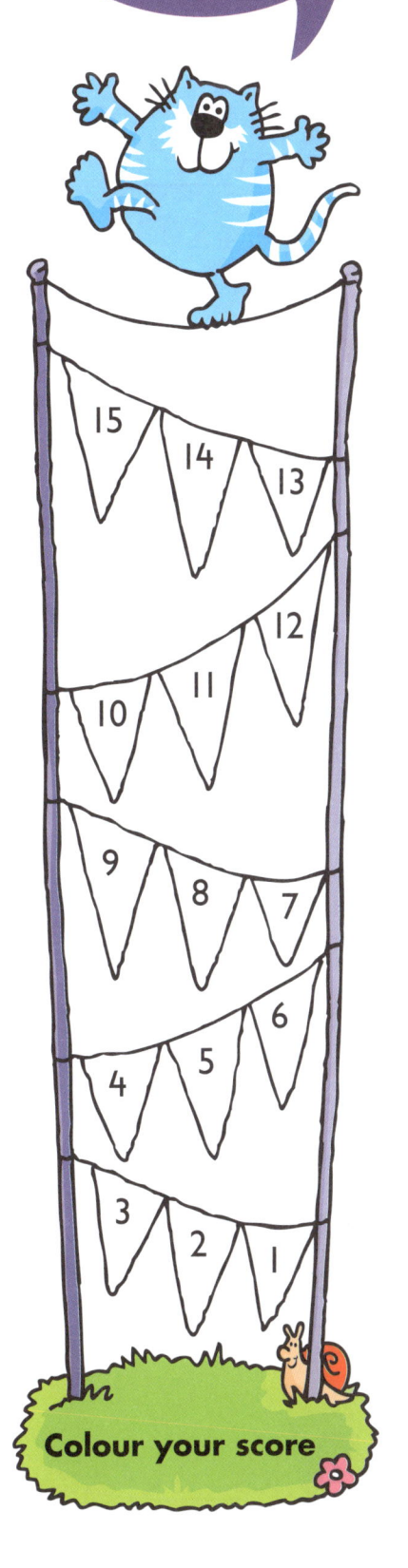

Colour your score

ng or nk?

Add **ng** or **nk** to the end to make a word.

n and **k** are two separate sounds that are often used together.

1. lu____
2. so____
3. chu____
4. alo____
5. bla____
6. dri____
7. sku____
8. ju____
9. ru____
10. dra____
11. fli____
12. li____
13. ga____
14. tru____
15. belo____

Colour your score

ck words

Write the word ending in ck next to each picture.

The first sound of each word has been done for you.

1. t _ _ _ _
2. b _ _ _ _
3. s _ _ _
4. s _ _ _ _
5. d _ _ _
6. qu _ _ _
7. c _ _ _ _
8. t _ _ _ t _ _ _
9. ch _ _ _
10. s _ _ _
11. c _ _ _ _
12. n _ _ _

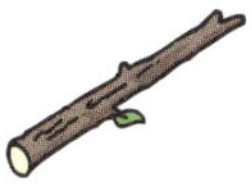

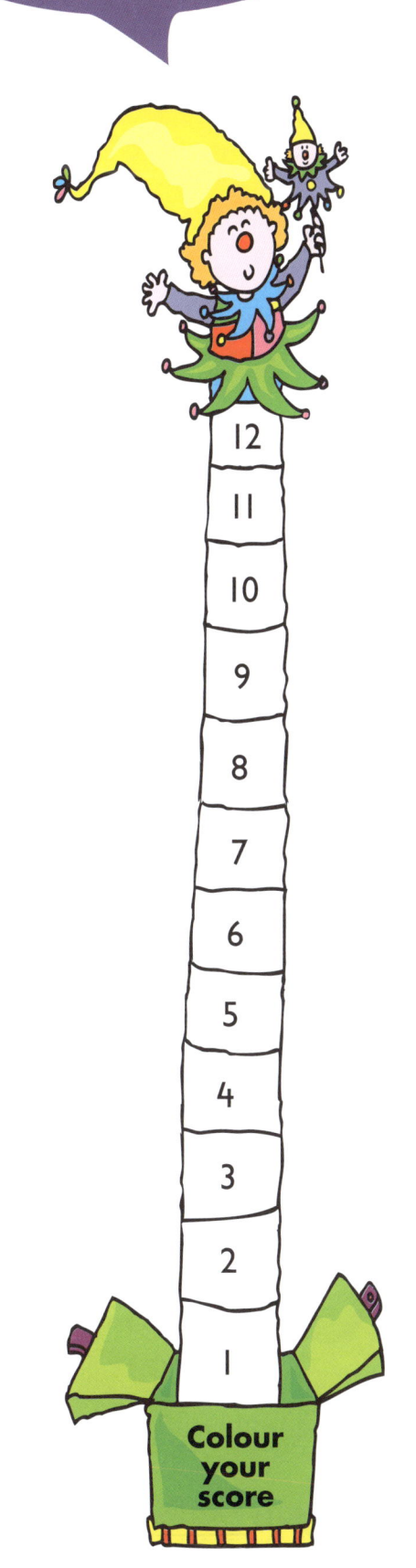

Colour your score

11

The long e sound

Choose ee or ea to fill the gap and make a word.

> ee and ea can both make the long e sound.

1. m____n
2. n____d
3. t____th
4. l____p
5. b____k
6. s____d
7. st____p
8. ____ch
9. s____l
10. qu____n
11. str____m
12. b____f
13. j____p
14. cl____n
15. betw____n

Colour your score

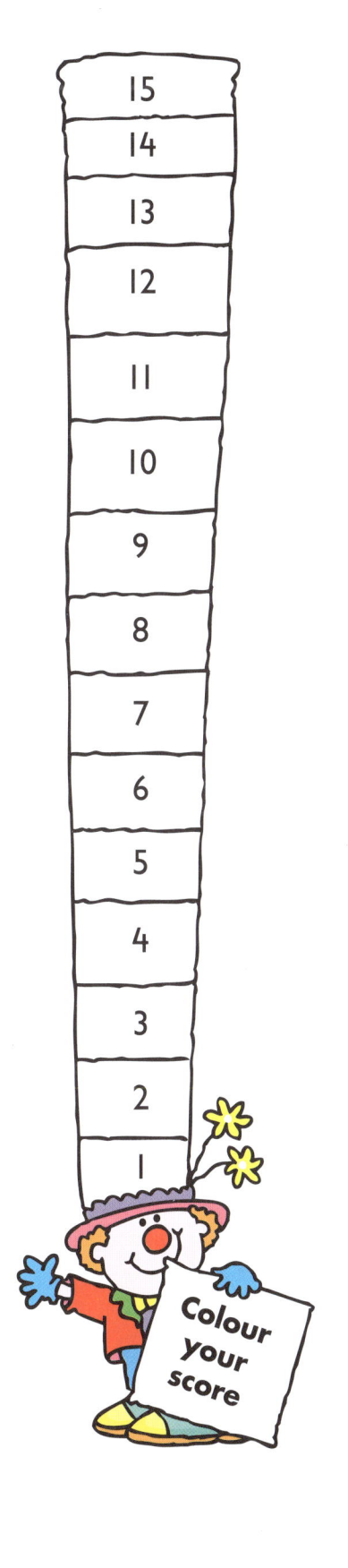

ss or zz?

Add ss or zz at the end to make a word.

1. le____
2. bu____
3. mo____
4. la____
5. lo____
6. fi____
7. ki____
8. bo____
9. mi____
10. ja____
11. cro____
12. hi____
13. to____
14. me____
15. whi____

There are more words ending with ss than with zz.

Colour your score

Rhyming pairs

Draw lines to link the pairs of words that rhyme.

Words that rhyme sometimes have different spellings.

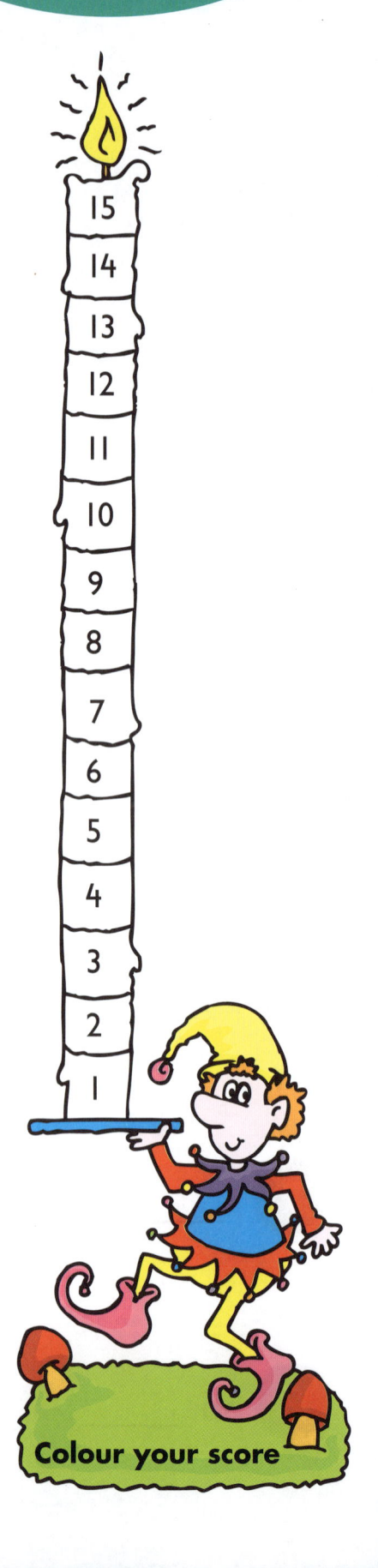

1. back — sink
2. long — kite
3. link — song
4. dash — sack
5. fight — smash
6. hutch — moon
7. pest — grand
8. soon — jet
9. yet — much
10. band — dressed
11. buzz — fell
12. hiss — stock
13. tell — miss
14. clock — hay
15. they — fuzz

Colour your score

ll or ff?

Add ll or ff at the end to make a word.

> l and f are often doubled at the end of words.

1. we____
2. flu____
3. o____
4. pi____
5. sme____
6. fri____
7. i____
8. she____
9. a____
10. do____
11. stu____
12. spi____
13. sni____
14. swe____
15. cli____

Colour your score

ou or ow?

Fill the gap with ou or ow to make a word.

1. d____n
2. m____th
3. c____
4. h____l
5. f____nd
6. cl____n
7. ____l
8. l____d
9. ab____t
10. h____
11. br____n
12. s____nd
13. pr____d
14. t____n
15. ar____nd

ou isn't usually at the end of a word.

Colour your score

f or ph?

Fill each gap with f or ph to make a word to match the picture.

Remember that f and ph sound the same.

1. ____rog 
2. ele____ant 
3. ____easant 
4. ____ox 
5. dol____in 
6. ____ish 
7. tele____one 
8. ____ence 
9. al____abet 
10. ____ork 
11. ____oto 
12. ____irework 
13. s____ere 
14. ____ossil 
15. ____an

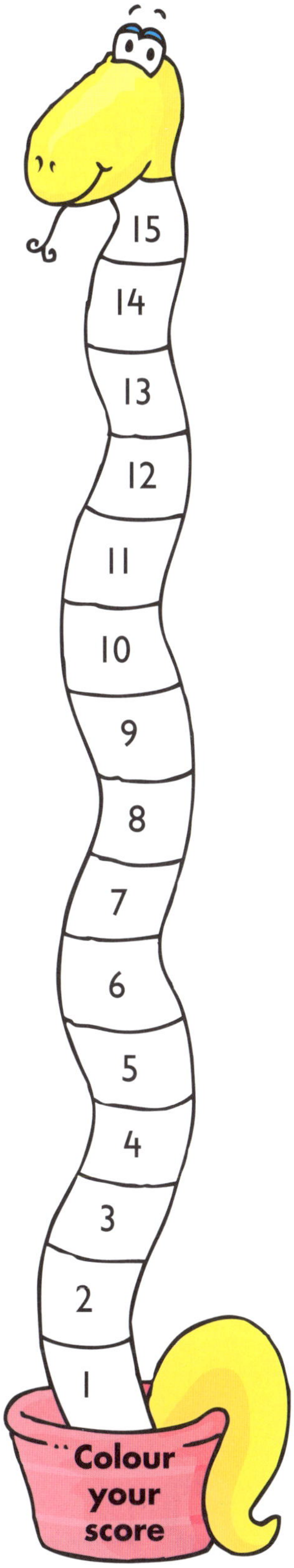

Colour your score

oi or oy?

Write **oi** or **oy** in the gap to make a word.

1. b____
2. b____l
3. c____n
4. t____
5. ____nk
6. enj____
7. destr____
8. j____nt
9. n____sy
10. r____al
11. m____st
12. ann____
13. cowb____
14. p____nt
15. s____l

oy is usually at the end of a word.

Colour your score

Rhyming words

Underline the word that rhymes with the word in purple.

> Words that rhyme sound the same at the end.

1. **sand** — land — lamp — sack
2. **sling** — slip — bring — brink
3. **light** — link — line — white
4. **cook** — cool — shook — shock
5. **seen** — clean — seat — sent
6. **long** — log — sock — song
7. **track** — smack — small — train
8. **toy** — coin — soil — boy
9. **will** — milk — chill — wheel
10. **think** — stink — this — thin
11. **catch** — much — witch — hatch
12. **jump** — jug — thump — thud
13. **he** — him — three — then
14. **nest** — met — pest — cress
15. **fox** — mix — fish — socks

Colour your score

Which grapheme?

Finish each word using the correct letters.

igh or i_e?

Don't forget the missing letter in **i_e** and **o_e**!

1. p_____ 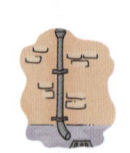
2. br_____ 
3. kn_____t 
4. l_____t 
5. b_____ 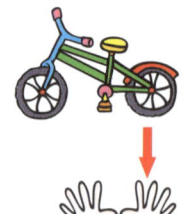 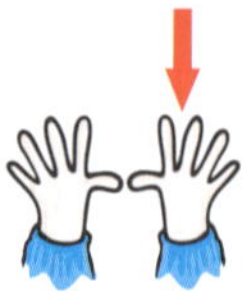
6. r_____t

oa or o_e?

7. g_____ 
8. ph_____ 
9. r_____ 
10. s_____ 
11. b_____ 
12. n_____

Colour your score

Words ending in y

Sort the words into two groups.

silly	by	my	happy
cry	funny	spotty	sky
dry	why	sunny	fry
	messy	fizzy	try

Words where y sounds like eye	Words where y sounds like ee

y at the end of words can sound like eye or ee.

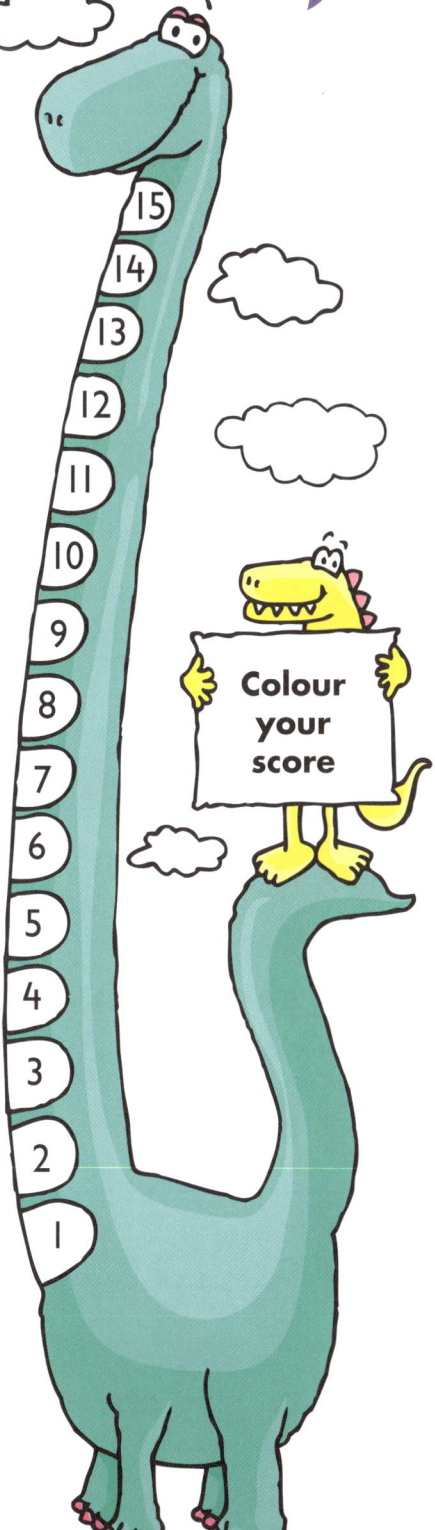

Colour your score

Which grapheme?

Finish each word using the correct letters.

ai or a_e?

1. c_____
2. tr_____
3. g_____
4. sn_____
5. ch_____
6. wh_____

ur or er?

7. p____son
8. ch____ch
9. n____se
10. c____l
11. p____se
12. m____maid

Don't forget to write the missing letter in a_e!

Colour your score

Vowel sounds after w

Add a, or or ar to make words.

You must use the same letter(s) for all the words in each set.

Try the letter(s) in all five words before you decide.

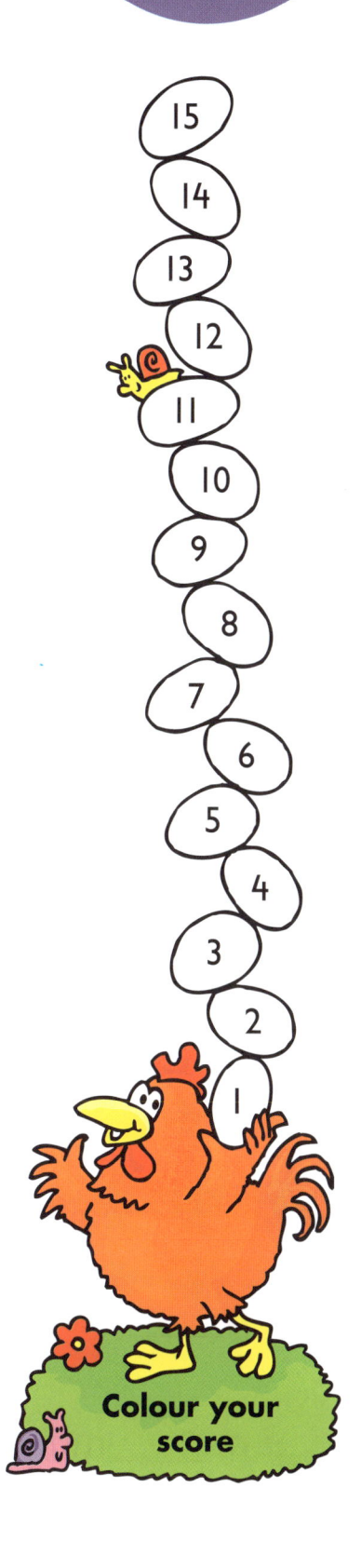

1. w_____nt
2. w_____tch
3. w_____nder
4. w_____nd
5. sw_____n

6. w_____d
7. w_____k
8. w_____m
9. w_____ld
10. w_____st

11. w_____
12. w_____m
13. tow_____ds
14. aw_____d
15. sw_____m

Colour your score

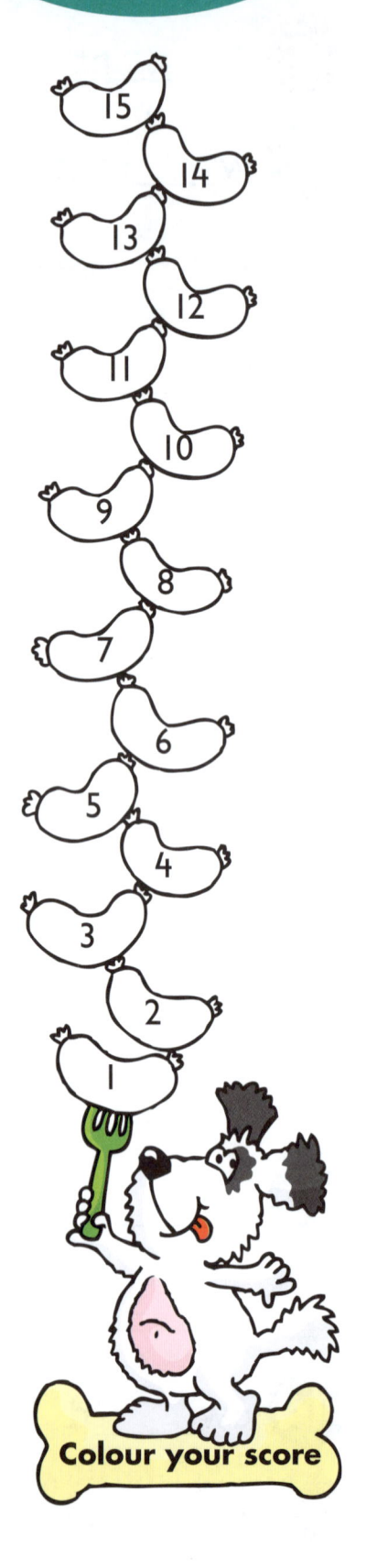

Silent letters

Add **wr, kn** or **gn** to make a word.

Check your answers by saying the words out loud. The w, k and g are silent.

1. ____ot
2. ____aw
3. ____ite
4. ____ife
5. ____ew
6. rei____
7. ____iggle
8. desi____
9. ____ote
10. ____estle
11. ____ee
12. ____ap
13. ____ats
14. ____ob
15. si____

Colour your score

The letter c

Sort the words into two groups.

cap	cottage	race	icy
carrot	cell	crab	clap
cylinder	close	fancy	century
coat	face	catch	

When c is before e, i or y, it makes an s sound.

c sounds like k, e.g. cat	c sounds like s, e.g. city

Colour your score

el, le or al?

Add el, le or al to make a word.

1. met____
2. tab____
3. jew____
4. ped____
5. lev____
6. squirr____
7. ank____
8. capit____
9. haz____
10. hospit____
11. bott____
12. midd____
13. tins____
14. fin____
15. litt____

The **el** spelling is less common than **le**.

Colour your score

ge or dge?

Write ge or dge to make a word.

1. ra____
2. bu____
3. wa____
4. bar____
5. ju____
6. do____
7. ga____t
8. sta____
9. a____
10. ri____
11. we____
12. pa____
13. le____
14. gor____
15. e____

ge and dge make the same sound.

Colour your score

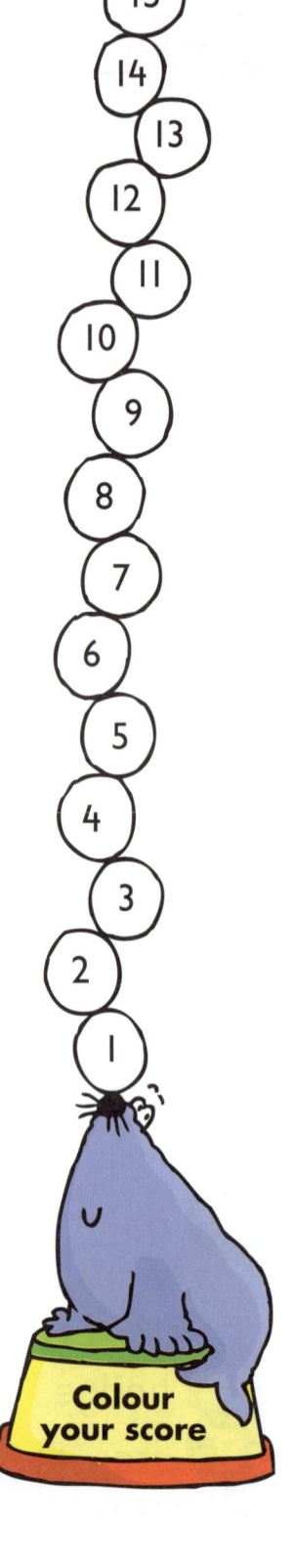

Word endings: y or ey

Write y or ey at the end to make a word.

Read the clue first.

1. An animal that lives in trees — monk____
2. A group of soldiers — arm____
3. Someone who rides racehorses — jock____
4. A new born child — bab____
5. A toy bear — tedd____
6. A crop grown in a field — barl____
7. An animal you can ride — donk____
8. Silly, wild, mad — craz____
9. An organ inside your body — kidn____
10. You buy things with this — mon____
11. Used to carry shopping — troll____
12. Fond of giving orders — boss____
13. Always curious about people — nos____
14. Another word for woman — lad____
15. Your stomach — tumm____

Colour your score

Compound words

Draw lines to join pairs of words that make longer words.

A compound word is made up of two shorter words.

1. tea — nut
2. back — stick
3. chest — bow
4. rain — pot
5. drum — pack
6. jelly — corn
7. pea — ship
8. pop — fish
9. space — light
10. spot — nut
11. tree — night
12. up — hog
13. wind — top
14. hedge — set
15. good — mill

Colour your score

a sounding 'or'

Write the word that matches each clue.

call	football	hall	tall
small	all	nightfall	wall
stall	fall	snowfall	waterfall

In all these words, a sounds like or.

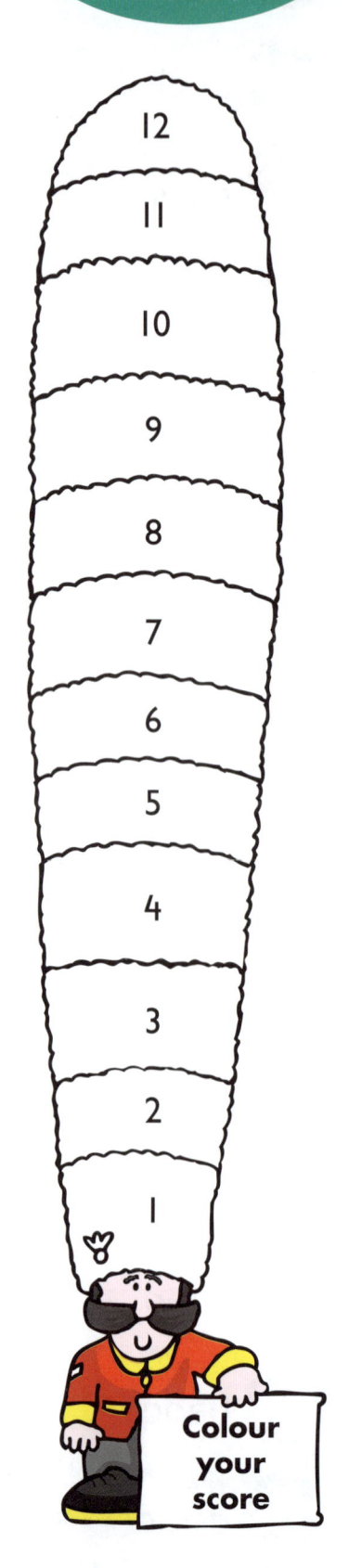

1. When it gets dark _____
2. A round object you kick _____
3. The opposite of short _____
4. Little _____
5. Everything _____
6. Made of bricks _____
7. To shout out _____
8. To tumble over _____
9. An entrance to a house _____
10. White flakes from the sky _____
11. A river flowing over a cliff _____
12. A table for selling in a market _____

Colour your score

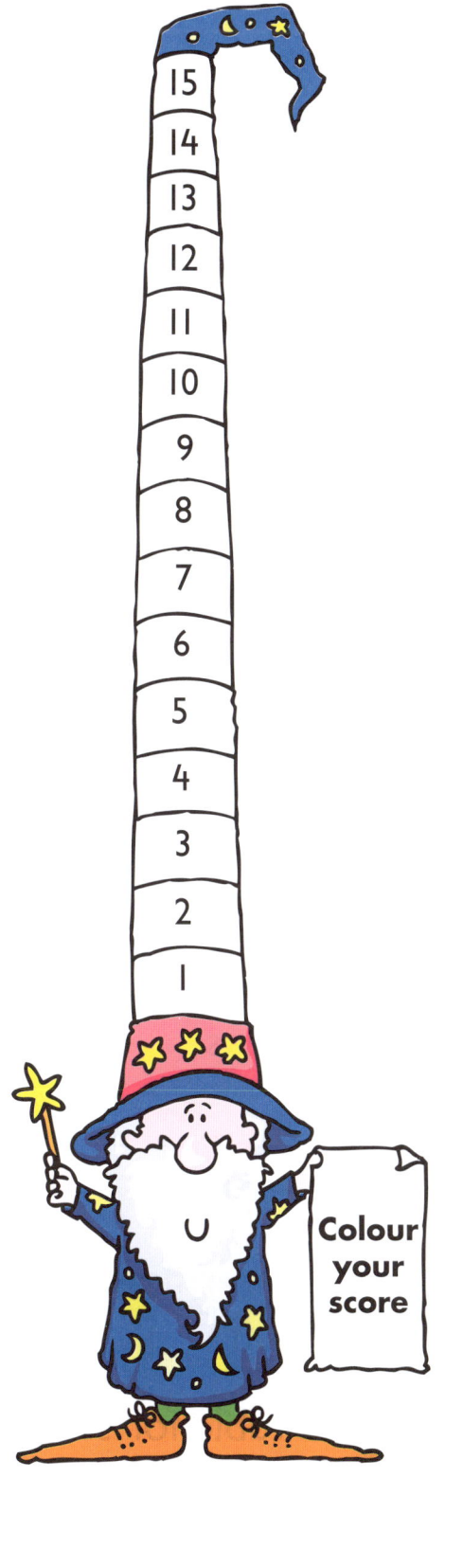

Choose an ending

Choose an ending to make a real word.

st, nk or sh?

mp, ck or ng?

Check each word by reading it out loud after writing.

1. bli____
2. fro____
3. bru____
4. tru____
5. tha____
6. sma____
7. dri____
8. fre____
9. fro____
10. qua____
11. alo____
12. thu____
13. bla____
14. swu____
15. ju____

Colour your score

Answers

Missing vowels
1. cat
2. dog
3. zip
4. log
5. hat
6. cap
7. cup
8. ten
9. sun
10. bed
11. fox
12. jam

Missing last sound
1. lid
2. mop
3. web
4. dish
5. sack
6. toy
7. fork
8. shed
9. rug
10. ship
11. map
12. well
13. sheep
14. ring
15. wood

x or cks?
1. mix
2. jinx
3. smacks
4. kicks
5. box
6. pecks
7. relax
8. lynx
9. tax / tacks
10. quacks
11. fix
12. suffix
13. ox
14. licks
15. backs

ch, sh or th?
1. them
2. chess
3. shut
4. shed
5. chap
6. thud
7. three
8. shall
9. chimp
10. shoot
11. this
12. than
13. chart
14. then

The short e sound
1. meant
2. hen
3. instead
4. spread
5. jet
6. web
7. head
8. yet
9. bread / bred
10. ten
11. thread
12. dead
13. lemon
14. nest
15. leg

oo words
1.–6. oo makes a short sound, e.g. look:
book, took, foot, wood, good, cook (in any order)

7.–15. oo makes a long sound, e.g. spoon:
food, pool, moon, zoo, mood, soon, bamboo, boom, broom (in any order)

or, ore, aw and au
1. more
2. short
3. born
4. score
5. before
6. horse
7. shore
8. saw
9. draw
10. author
11. pause
12. yawn
13. astronaut
14. crawl
15. haunt

Word endings
1. bank
2. lock
3. crust
4. sap
5. well
6. wish
7. park
8. honk
9. meet
10. hulk
11. book
12. boat
13. desk
14. thank
15. sheep

ng or nk?
1. lung
2. song
3. chunk
4. along
5. blank
6. drink
7. skunk
8. junk
9. rung
10. drank
11. fling
12. link
13. gang
14. trunk
15. belong

ck words
1. truck
2. brick
3. sack
4. stick
5. duck
6. quack
7. clock
8. tick tock
9. chick
10. sock
11. cluck
12. neck

The long e sound
1. mean
2. need
3. teeth
4. leap
5. beak
6. seed
7. steep
8. each
9. seal
10. queen
11. stream
12. beef
13. jeep
14. clean
15. between

ss or zz?
1. less
2. buzz
3. moss
4. lass
5. loss
6. fizz
7. kiss
8. boss
9. miss
10. jazz
11. cross
12. hiss
13. toss
14. mess
15. whizz

Rhyming pairs
1. back + sack
2. long + song
3. link + sink
4. dash + smash
5. fight + kite
6. hutch + much
7. pest + dressed
8. soon + moon
9. yet + jet
10. band + grand
11. buzz + fuzz
12. hiss + miss
13. tell + fell
14. clock + stock
15. they + hay

ll or ff?
1. well
2. fluff
3. off
4. pill
5. smell
6. frill
7. ill
8. shell
9. all
10. doll / doff
11. stuff
12. spill
13. sniff
14. swell
15. cliff

ou or ow?
1. down
2. mouth
3. cow
4. howl
5. found
6. clown
7. owl
8. loud
9. about
10. how
11. brown
12. sound
13. proud
14. town
15. around

f or ph?
1. frog
2. elephant
3. pheasant
4. fox
5. dolphin
6. fish
7. telephone
8. fence
9. alphabet
10. fork
11. photo
12. firework
13. sphere
14. fossil
15. fan